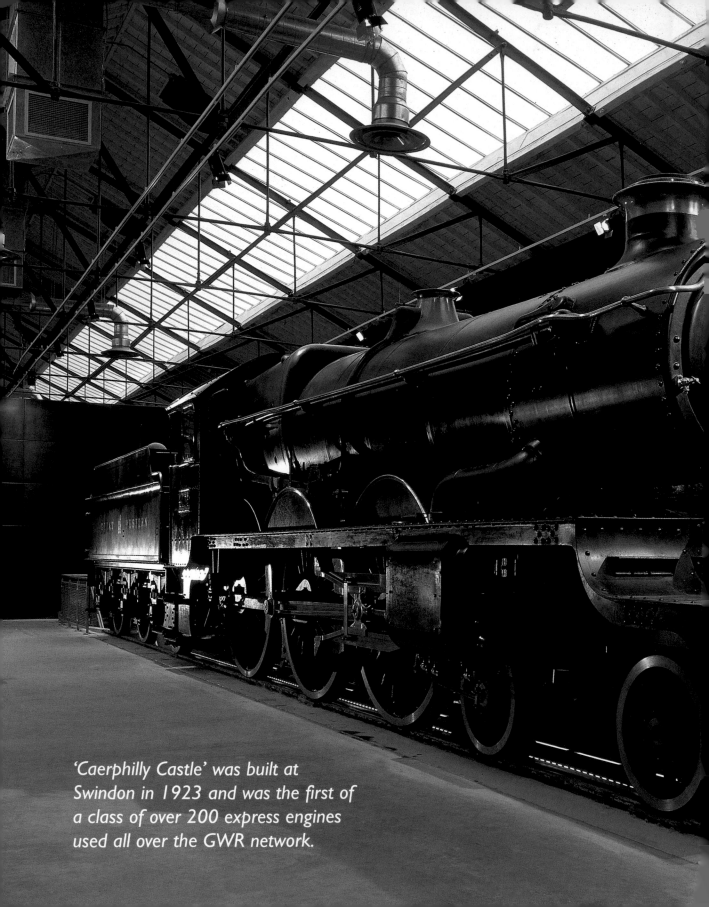

'Caerphilly Castle' was built at
Swindon in 1923 and was the first of
a class of over 200 express engines
used all over the GWR network.

Welcome to STEAM

Museum of The Great Western Railway, Swindon

STEAM - Museum of the Great Western Railway, opened to the public on 14 June 2000 and celebrates the remarkable story of the men and women who built, operated and travelled on 'God's Wonderful Railway'.

We hope that you will enjoy your day out at **STEAM** as we take you on a journey into the heart of the Great Western Railway at Swindon, which in its heyday dominated the fortunes of the town and the railway it served. Swindon was famous as a place where some of the best steam locomotives in the world were built, and our Museum gives visitors the chance to experience the sights and sounds of the railway works, and to hear the stories of the men and women who worked there.

Away from the workshops at Swindon, the story of the Great Western Railway is also brought to life from the exploits of its flamboyant engineer, Isambard Kingdom Brunel, to the running of a great enterprise like the GWR, which employed over 70,000 staff at its peak.

Our Museum has been made possible through the support of the Heritage Lottery Fund, Swindon Borough Council, Carillion Development Management and BAA McArthurGlen, and the National Railway Museum at York.

We are proud of **STEAM** and hope that you enjoy your visit and come again!

Contents

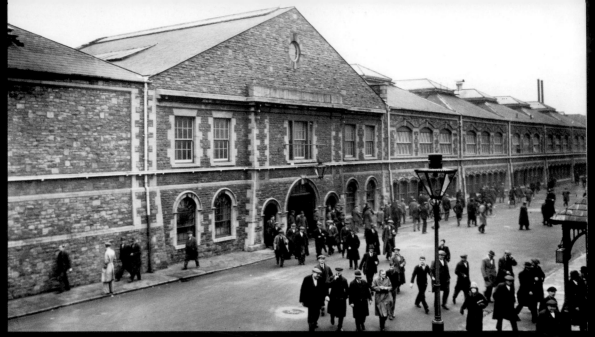

Men stream from the famous 'Tunnel Entrance' of the works at the end of a shift in the 1930s.

Swindon Works

The decision to site the Great Western Railway's workshops at Swindon was made in 1841 when the Board of Directors authorised construction of 'an establishment commensurate with the wants of the company'. Isambard Kingdom Brunel and Daniel Gooch, the Locomotive Superintendent, had visited Swindon in 1840 and had chosen a site at the junction of the branch line to Cheltenham and the Great Western main line to Bristol.

The area chosen was some distance from the old town of Swindon, in green fields a short distance from the Wilts and Berks canal. As well as already being a railway junction, Swindon was also the place where it was planned to change locomotives on Bristol-London trains, since west of the town Brunel's railway scaled severe gradients, including

the 1 in 100 of the Wootton Bassett Incline and the tunnel at Box.

The Works opened in January 1843 but was only a repair and maintenance facility in its early years. By 1846 however, it had turned out its first engine - 'The Great Western' - starting a long tradition of locomotive manufacture on the site.

Further expansion took place in 1868 when the Carriage and Wagon Works was opened at Swindon. In the years before 1900 the Works grew steadily. With the turn of a new century a dynamic new Locomotive Superintendent, George Jackson Churchward, transformed the Works into a modern factory. Old equipment was replaced and new workshops, particularly the huge 'A'

Erecting Shop, were built, making Swindon one of the biggest and best-equipped railway workshops in the world.

After the First World War, the expansion slowed, but even so, by 1935 the Works covered an area of 326 acres, 73 of which were roofed. After 1945 the Works took some time to recover from the demands placed on it during the Second World War.

In the Second World War the adaptability and ingenuity of Swindon staff was called on time and time again as the Works produced all manner of items for the war effort. The workshops became a munitions factory, producing shell and bomb cases, but it also built tanks, landing craft, and midget submarines. The War also saw the introduction of female staff, who came into the factory to replace men drafted into the services, working in every part of the Works.

After the nationalisation of the railways in 1948, locomotives built to Swindon designs continued to be produced, but there was a gradual decline in the fortunes of the Works, marked by the production of the last steam locomotive for British Railways, 'Evening Star' in 1960. In 1963, a large part of the Carriage Works was closed and Works activity was concentrated on the area west of the Cheltenham line. The end of diesel locomotive production proved to be the final straw, and despite some resurgence in the 1970s, the closure of the Works seemed inevitable.

Men testing the support fixings of a 250lb bomb at Swindon Works during the Second World War. The Works manufactured a variety of bombs and shells for the war effort in both world wars.

A female boilersmith inside the smokebox of a Great Western engine in the Boiler Shop in 1943.

The end finally came in 1986 when British Rail Engineering Limited finally closed the Works after 143 years of operation.

The closure of the workshops left a core of important industrial buildings, and developers Carillion have undertaken a programme of refurbishment and restoration, with its partners, to give them new uses. In 1995 the old Works Managers Offices were formally opened as the headquarters of the National Monuments Record Centre (part of English Heritage), and two years later, the old Boiler Shop complex was converted into the Great Western Designer Outlet Village - a large shopping centre set within the old railway workshops. As well as **STEAM**, further developments are taking place to complete the restoration of this historic site.

The Museum Building

Like many buildings on the old Swindon Works site, the Museum has a complex history.

The entrance area, known as the 'Scraggery' to Swindon staff, was built in 1846 as part of the original Brunel Works, and consisted of a two-storey machine shop. What is now the Storehouse exhibition area was a blacksmiths shop, built at the same time. In 1865, a separate building, the 'R' Machine Shop was built, but the space between the two was not roofed until 1872. Further alterations were made between 1929 and 1931 when the offices on the north side of the building were added. To the south, next to the main line,

an extension to the building and the adjoining 'B' Shop was made. In 1967, the workshop was gutted, renamed '20' Shop, and converted into a wheel shop. After closure in 1986, the workshop was used as a restoration workshop.

The Museum building was a Machine Shop for most of its life. Staff are working on a variety of machines in this 1950s view of the workshop.

The Locomotive Works

A Hawksworth 'County' Class locomotive being run on the Locomotive Test Plant. Engines could be run at speeds up to 80mph on this machine, nicknamed the 'Home Trainer' by staff.

The workshops at Swindon were divided into two sections - the Locomotive Works and the Carriage and Wagon Works. Each had their own character, and the staff employed there needed quite different skills in many cases.

The construction of a Great Western Railway locomotive involved a large number of staff and workshops providing component parts for final assembly in the Erecting Shop, where the finished product was finally built.

The process began in the offices. With 12,000 staff, and many tasks and operations to manage and account for, a complex bureaucracy was required. Hundreds of clerks were employed and in many cases, information was laboriously recorded in ledgers by hand. Women were first employed in the offices during the First World War, altering the male dominated atmosphere for good. Even after the war women continued to be employed in the offices, although they were expected to resign when they married!

At the start of the physical process of locomotive construction were the 'hot' shops. In the Foundry, ferrous and non-ferrous castings were made, and in the Steam Hammer Shop, drop or steam hammers were used to forge large items like connecting rods, or to stamp out forgings to the correct profile.

The Museum building was one of a series of machine shops situated around the works. Here metal components could be shaped and turned to the correct size, ready for fitting onto locomotives, by machines such as lathes, drills, grinders, planers or slotters.

One of the many women employed in the works during the Second World War, polishing locomotive connecting rods in the 'A' Shop.

Rivet hotting was a dirty and hazardous job. A hydraulic riveting machine is being used, but neither of the staff in this wartime picture wears any ear protection.

Before the advent of electricity, machines were belt driven, with stationary steam locomotives situated outside each workshop to supply the power to drive them. The Machine Shop display in the Museum features a number of belt driven machines that have been restored by the Friends of Swindon Railway Museum. The oldest, a bevel gear cutter, dates back to 1887.

The noisiest workshop was without doubt the Boiler Shop. Here boilers were assembled and repaired, and the din of hundreds of men using hydraulic riveters, welding machines and hammers was tremendous. No wonder most boilersmiths were deaf by the age of thirty! There were also a multitude of other specialist workshops producing parts. The familiar brass domes or safety valve covers were made in the 'K' Shop, whilst the Spring Shop made both leaf and coil springs. When the Works closed in 1986 the production methods had changed little in a century or more. In the 'T' Shop, whistles, safety valves, buffers and other items were made before being sent through to the Erecting Shop, where they could be fitted onto new or repaired locomotives.

The great 'A' Erecting Shop was a huge building dedicated to the final assembly of locomotives. Completed in 1921, it was the place where the locomotive jigsaw was finally completed, although heavy repairs were also carried out there. With the aid of two 100 ton cranes, locomotives could be easily moved around the workshop. When an engine was finally completed, it could be taken out on trial on the main line, or could be run on the Locomotive Test Plant in the 'A' Shop, where static locomotives could be run up to 80mph.

The inside of the original 'A' Erecting Shop in 1904, not long after its completion. Note the large gas light hanging from the roof.

13

Swindon Locomotives

The locomotives built and operated by the Great Western Railway have always attracted great attention from engineers, enthusiasts and the general public, and there is not the space in a guide of this type to give a detailed description of the engines that made the company so famous.

The locomotives on display in the Museum provide a good cross section of Great Western motive power and show something of the variety of engines produced at Swindon.

When the Great Western Railway was planned, Brunel had intended to have locomotives for his new line built by manufacturers to specifications he produced. When, in 1837, the company appointed Daniel Gooch as its first locomotive superintendent, he discovered that Brunel's locomotives were a disaster. Known as 'Freaks', it was reported that these engines could hardly pull themselves along, let alone a train!

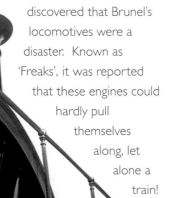

Fortunately, Gooch was able to obtain two engines from the Robert Stephenson Company that had been originally intended for a 5' 6" gauge railway in the United States. The scheme had failed, and Stephenson was happy to re-gauge them to Brunel's 7ft broad gauge. 'North Star' in the 'Building the Railway' section of the Museum, is a 1925 replica of the engine that became one of the first to run on the GWR in 1837. Although a replica, 'North Star' does give an insight into how early GWR locomotives looked and operated.

The high point of the broad gauge era was the 'Iron Duke' class 4-2-2 express engine that was built at Swindon from 1851 onwards. These graceful engines were the mainstay of express services, and survived after rebuilding, until the end of Brunel's broad gauge in 1892.

Gooch was succeeded by Joseph Armstrong as Locomotive Superintendent in 1864, and both he and William Dean, who took over in 1877, designed a wide range of locomotives for both broad and standard gauge use. The oldest locomotive in the collection is 0-6-0 'Dean Goods' built in 1897. William Dean's design is simple and robust, and this type of engine was used on coal trains and other goods working until it was relegated onto lighter duties with the introduction of more modern designs. Many of the class were used by the War Department during both World Wars, although No. 2516 was not taken overseas. It did have a very long working life, and was still active in the early 1950s before being taken out of service for preservation.

In 1837, 'North Star' became one of the first locomotives to run on the GWR. This 1925 replica can be seen in the 'Building the Railway' section.

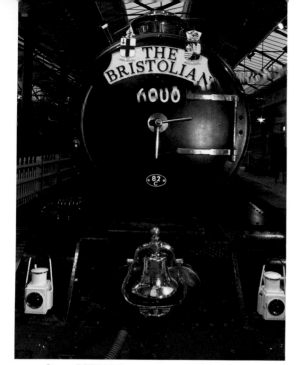

One of STEAM's most spectacular exhibits – 'King George V'

the benchmark for express passenger development between the two World Wars, and we are fortunate to have examples of both in our Museum.

'Caerphilly Castle' was built at Swindon in 1923 and was the first of a class of over 200 express engines used all over the GWR network. Number 6000 'King George V' built in 1927, is the flagship of the Great Western Railway, and achieved fame when it travelled to the United States in the same year for the Centenary Celebrations of the Baltimore & Ohio Railroad. It made such an impression that it was presented with the bell that is still mounted on its buffer beam.

George Jackson Churchward took over from Dean as Locomotive Superintendent in 1902 and produced designs for a stream of Great Western locomotives that were well ahead of their time, and were to influence GWR locomotive policy for the next 40 years. Churchward aimed to produce a complete set of standard locomotive designs from express passenger, heavy freight, mixed traffic and tank engines. As well as his famous 'Saint' and 'Star' express engines, he also introduced a number of tank locomotives including the 4200 2-8-0 class. The sole example of a Churchward design in the Museum is displayed in a skeletal form in our Erecting Shop displays. No. 4248, built at Swindon in 1916 was used for many years on coal trains in South Wales, as well as on china clay trains in Cornwall.

The work done by Churchward was expanded on by C.B. Collett, Chief Mechanical Engineer from 1922 to 1942. His 'Castle' and 'King' designs were

A front view of one of Daniel Gooch's broad gauge 4-2-2 express locomotives.

A view of one of the most famous GWR engines 'King George V', taken shortly after its return to England from the USA in 1927.

The last Chief Mechanical Engineer of the Great Western Railway was F.W. Hawksworth, who succeeded Collett in 1942. Wartime shortages and the need to concentrate on war work did not give him the opportunity to design large numbers of engines in the way his predecessors had done. Most successful were his 'County' class 4-6-0 express engines, none of which have been preserved. However, an example of his 1947 design of pannier tank locomotive No. 9400 is on display in the 'Great Western Goods' section of the Museum.

Many examples of this type of engine had been used on the GWR for several years, the term 'pannier' referring to the water tanks, on each side of the boiler, that resemble pannier bags.

After nationalisation, Swindon became part of the British Railways network, and the post of Chief Mechanical Engineer ceased to exist. Swindon maintained an independent policy on locomotive development, and tested and used two gas turbine locomotives before beginning to build diesel designs. These too used a different philosophy to that practised by other regions, since instead of constructing diesel electric designs, Swindon adopted diesel hydraulic locomotives, building a number of classes of locomotive including the 'Warship' and 'Western' engines. The end of locomotive production at Swindon in the 1960s appeared to be the end for the workshops, but there was a brief swansong in 1978, when Swindon built 20 diesel shunters for Kenyan railways, a fitting finale to a proud tradition dating back to 1846.

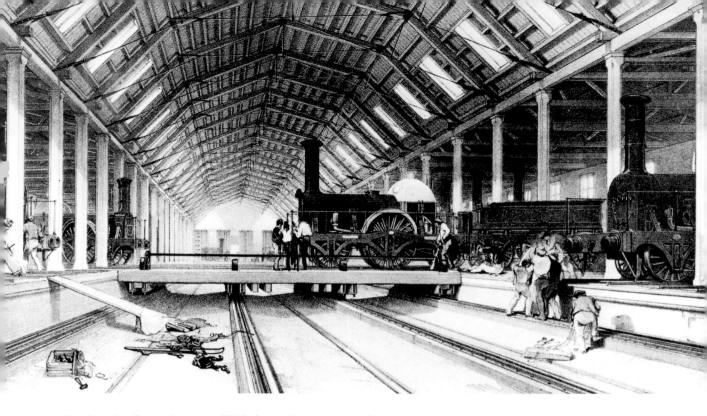

The Swindon Engine House in 1846, from a lithograph by J.C. Bourne.
One of Daniel Gooch's 'Firefly' class engines is receiving attention on the traverser.

GWR Blueprint Castle Class Locomotive

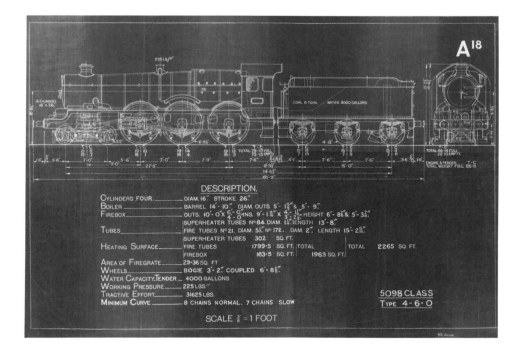

The Carriage Works

Covering an area of over 150 acres, the Carriage Works encompassed a wide variety of trades and skills, many much different to those employed by the Locomotive Department. The process of building carriages and wagons again consisted of a number of smaller workshops, all producing component parts for the finished product.

The Carriage Department had its own 'hot' shops, where steam or drop hammers were employed, as well as large blacksmiths' shops. Once produced, parts were taken to the fitting and machine shop where metal fittings, such as axle boxes, bogies, brake gear, door handles and other fittings were made. Wheel lathes were employed in 16 Shop where wheels were manufactured and refurbished. The metal tyres on wheels were re-profiled on

these lathes, and large hydraulic presses were used to press the wheels onto axles to the correct gauge.

Timber for the construction of carriages and wagons came from the Works Sawmill. Enormous logs were cut into more manageable sizes. Much of the timber used in the Great Western era is now endangered rainforest species. Mahogany, teak and other woods were used in the building of carriages. 'The origin of woods' interactive display in the Carriage Works section shows the range and geographical distribution of timber used by the railway. In the Finishing Shop, wood from the Sawmill was used to make carriage doors, windows, seat backs and other interior fittings. In the Trimming Shop, upholsterers and other craftsmen manufactured items such as seats, cushions and

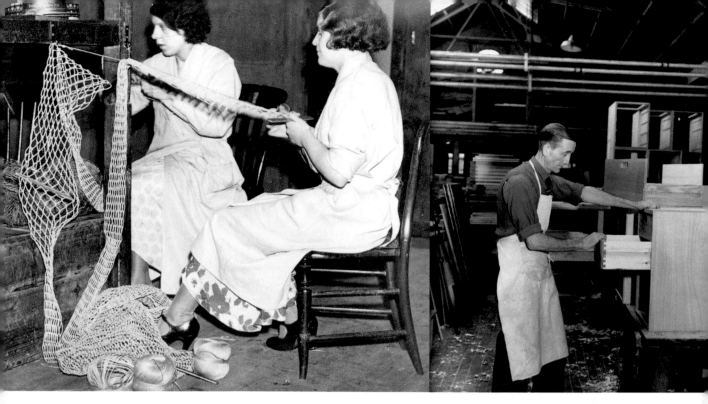

Above: Making carriage luggage rack nets in the Carriage Works in the 1920s. Female staff were employed in many parts of the Carriage Works, particularly in areas where skill and dexterity were required, such as the Trim Shop or the Upholsterers Shop. Above right: A carpenter at work building furniture in the Carriage Works. The GWR was in many ways self sufficient, providing itself with most of the furniture and equipment it needed.

luggage racks, as well as towels and bed linen used by the Hotels and Refreshment Departments.

The equivalent of the Locomotive Erecting Shop was the Carriage Body Shop. Carriages were assembled, underframes and bogies added before being painted, lettered and varnished. Many hundreds of hours of work were required before a carriage could be added to the company's stock. The carriage in our display is typical of those produced after the First World War. After this date carriages were built with sheet steel being attached to a timber framework, rather than the all-wood method adopted previously. In a separate workshop, the rather less glamorous task of wagon construction continued, and thousands of wagons of all types were built and repaired.

The Carriage Works also carried out a number of other more general jobs for the railway. In the Machine and Fitting Shop ticket machines were built and maintained, and in the Carpenters' Shop a huge variety of items in general use by staff were manufactured. Hand carts, platform seats, desks, chairs and other furniture were all built, all bearing the initials branded 'GWR'.

The Carriage Body Shop. A number of carriages are under repair. In the foreground is the carriage door handle exhibit now on display in the Carriage Shop section of **STEAM**.

Outside the Works

As the railway works expanded across the fields below the old town of Swindon, a whole community, known as New Swindon, was born next to the workshops.

There had been little tradition of heavy engineering in North Wiltshire, so most staff for the new works came from areas where railway engineering was already established such as Scotland, the North East of England and Manchester. The old town of Swindon could not cope with such an influx, and as a result, the Great Western Railway built what is now known as the Railway Village; an estate of 300 houses for its staff. Constructed by the London contractor J. D. & C. Rigby, who was also constructing Swindon Station, the village grew slowly, and by 1847 only 241 houses had been built. It was not until the 1860s that work was finally completed, but the standard of accommodation was rather better than industrial houses elsewhere. Even so, the cottages were overcrowded; one two-roomed house was recorded as having eleven inhabitants, man, wife, five children and four lodgers!

By the time the Village was completed, it was already too small, and streets of red brick houses grew up around the ever-expanding railway works. The town grew rapidly, and in 1900 the population of Old and New Swindon had reached over 40,000, growing to 65,000 in 1935.

As well as the village, a number of other organisations were an integral part of the railway community in Swindon. The Mechanics Institution began in 1843, as an attempt by the men themselves to set up their own library. Because of the lack of social and educational facilities in the new town, they also held dances and other events. Because they had no building, they used rooms in the Works, including the upstairs part of what is now the entrance to the Museum. By 1855 the Institution was big enough to have its own building in Emlyn Square. This had excellent facilities, with a theatre, library and meeting rooms, and became the cultural centre of the town.

In 1847, the Great Western Medical Fund was set up, initially to fund the provision of a doctor for the Village and the Works, since none was provided in the vicinity. With the assistance of Daniel Gooch, the Locomotive Superintendent, the railway funded half the salary of a doctor. The workmen raised the rest of the money themselves.

This arrangement continued, and the Medical Fund soon grew up into a superb 'Cradle to Grave' medical service, with doctors, dentists, opticians, public baths and a pharmacy. The new Medical Fund headquarters, built in 1892, also included two swimming pools and Turkish baths. With this

The Coat of Arms of the Borough of Swindon (1900 to 1974). The locomotive featured was Dean 4-2-2 'White Horse' (No 3029).

A view of the Railway Village in the 1860s. Steam can be seen rising from the Railway Works.

standard of care it was no wonder that the National Health Service drew much of its inspiration from developments at Swindon.

Unlike some other model village schemes set up in the Victorian period, the Great Western Railway did not insist on staff attending church. Provision was made for the spiritual welfare of the men however, with the construction of St. Marks church in 1845. Close to the church was the GWR School opened soon after the Works itself in 1843. Opposite the church was the GWR Park, originally known as the 'Plantation'. It is rumoured that W.G. Grace, the famous cricketer, played there, although the park was better known by Swindon people as the place where the annual GWR Fete was held. Eagerly looked forward to every year, thousands crowded into the park with children receiving a piece of special fruit-cake, and tickets for two rides on the fairground which was always provided.

The Mechanics Institute in Emlyn Square, Swindon, after the building was extended in 1893.

A reconstruction of the opening of the GWR in 1838, when the London to Maidenhead section was finally completed.

Building The Great Western Railway

The success of early lines like the Stockton & Darlington Railway, opened in 1825, and the Liverpool and Manchester Railway, opened in 1830, played an important part in persuading the business community in Bristol that a rail link to London was essential if it was to remain an important centre for business and industry. After some discussion, a committee was formed in 1833 to set up a railway, and one of its first tasks was to appoint an engineer for the new line. The man they chose was Isambard Kingdom Brunel, a young engineer who had come to prominence in the city by winning a competition to design a suspension bridge over the River Avon at Clifton.

Brunel's first task was to survey a route for the line, and by August 1833 enough work had been done to issue a prospectus for the new company, now to be named the Great Western Railway. There was considerable opposition to the railway, not least from the Provost of Eton College, who thought that the line would be 'injurious to the discipline of the school and dangerous to the morals of pupils'. Two attempts were needed to get the scheme through parliament, but on 31 August 1835 Royal Assent was finally granted, allowing work to begin.

Work started almost immediately on construction of the 112 mile line, which, it was estimated, would

This reconstruction took place in 1935 for a film made to celebrate the company's centenary.

cost £2,500,000. Brunel had a very strong idea of the railway he wanted.

It would not be a copy of schemes already built or under construction but would be a whole railway system, with its own unique buildings, track, track gauge and motive power. Working long hours, Brunel supervised almost every aspect of the project, producing drawings and specifications, meeting with landowners and contractors, and checking work as it progressed.

The construction of the railway was divided into many separate contracts for particular stretches of line or structures like bridges, each carried out by a particular contractor employing gangs of navvies to do the construction work. Unlike today, railways like the Great Western were built largely by sheer physical effort, and railway builders had few machines to help them. The navvies were, without

The interior of Box Tunnel in 1846.

A plan of the original GWR line from the company prospectus issued in 1834.

doubt, a tough breed, who worked hard for relatively poor pay in bad conditions. Many lived in tented shantytowns dotted along the route of the railway, and their drinking and behaviour struck terror in the hearts of local communities.

The route of the railway between London and Bristol ran along the Thames Valley from London to Reading, crossing the river a number of times, most notably at Maidenhead, where Brunel's graceful bridge caused much controversy due to the shallowness of its arches.

From Reading to Swindon, the line runs along what is now nicknamed 'Brunel's Billiard Table' because of its easy gradients. After Swindon however, the railway is forced to cross a far more hilly landscape, and the route includes some ferocious gradients of 1 in 100 at Wootton Bassett and through Box Tunnel. The tunnel at Box was another cause of

controversy, burrowing through two miles of Cotswold limestone, it was one of the last sections of the railway to be completed, and only one track was ready for use when the Great Western Railway finally opened throughout from London to Bristol on 30 June 1841.

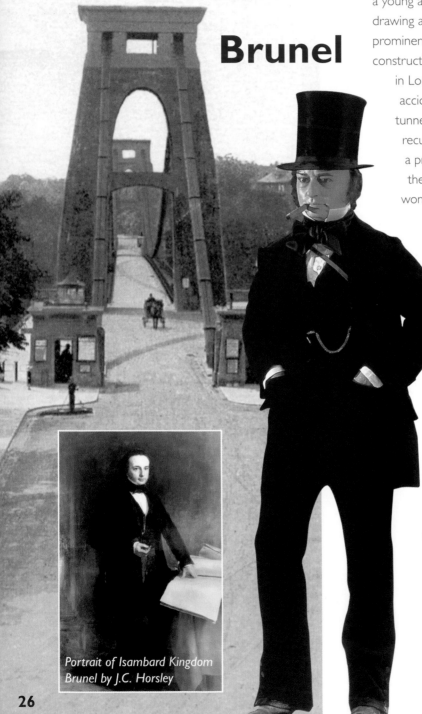

The Clifton Suspension Bridge over the River Avon, Bristol; Brunel's first major project and one not completed in his lifetime.

Brunel

Portrait of Isambard Kingdom Brunel by J.C. Horsley

Born on 9th April 1806, Isambard Kingdom Brunel was one of the most famous and flamboyant of the Victorian engineers. His father, Marc Isambard Brunel was also a distinguished engineer, and from a young age IKB showed a precocious talent for drawing and mathematics. He first came to prominence working with his father on the construction of a tunnel under the River Thames in London in 1827. Badly injured in an accident during the construction of the tunnel, Isambard was sent to Bristol to recuperate, and it was here that he heard of a project to design a suspension bridge over the River Avon at Clifton. Brunel eventually won a competition to design the bridge, and although it was not completed in his lifetime, it was a springboard for his career. Whilst in Bristol he heard of plans to build a new railway from London to Bristol, and in 1833 he was appointed as engineer of the Great Western Railway.

He also designed many other railways including the Bristol & Exeter, the South Devon, South Wales, and the Cornwall and West Cornwall Railways. Some of his drawing and surveying equipment can be seen in the showcase near to the tunnel in the Museum.

Not all Brunel's work was entirely successful. The use of the controversial 'Atmospheric' system in the construction of the South Devon Railway was one of his more conspicuous failures - George

Stephenson called it a 'humbug' and the system never really worked, leaving the shareholders of the railway with a large loss. The timber viaducts he designed, many of which were used in the West Country were cheap to build, but had a short life span, and eventually had to be replaced by the GWR at considerable cost.

A model of the Ponsonooth Viaduct near Truro is displayed near the 'North Star' locomotive. Elsewhere however, many of Brunel's successful railway accomplishments survive - Paddington Station, Maidenhead Bridge, Bristol Temple Meads Station and, perhaps his greatest achievement, the Royal Albert Bridge over the River Tamar at Saltash, opened in 1859.

Brunel was also an accomplished marine engineer, and designed three steamships. The 'Great Western', launched in 1838, was a conventional wooden hulled paddle steamer, but its successor, the 'Great Britain', was revolutionary in many ways. It was the first iron-hulled, screw propeller driven Atlantic liner, and, but for an unfortunate wreck some years after its launch in 1843, would have been a great success. The Great Western Steamship Company, that had built the ship, ran out of money, and the 'Great Britain' was sold, being rebuilt to transport passengers to and from Australia, which it did for many years. Brunel's third ship, the 'Great Eastern', launched in 1859, was a far different proposition. This huge ship, designed to sail from England to Australia, weighed more than 18,000 tons, and its construction and launch were fraught with difficulties, hastening the death, in 1859, of the great engineer. Brunel also designed a prefabricated hospital for the Crimean War, assisted in the Crystal Palace exhibition of 1851, and many other projects besides.

A cartoon from 'Punch' marking the end of Brunel's broad gauge. Brunel's ghost haunts the scene.

The launch of the 'SS Great Britain' in Bristol in 1843.

The 'SS Great Eastern', Brunel's third steamship design.

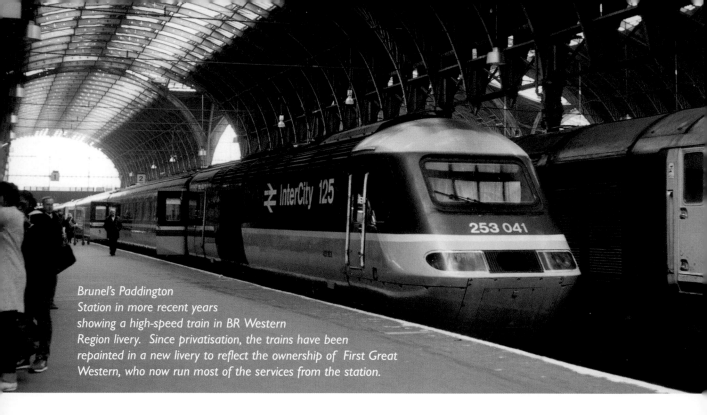

Brunel's Paddington Station in more recent years showing a high-speed train in BR Western Region livery. Since privatisation, the trains have been repainted in a new livery to reflect the ownership of First Great Western, who now run most of the services from the station.

The Growth of the Network

Brunel's original Great Western Railway was to link the two cities of Bristol and London, and the company coat of arms reflects this, incorporating the arms of both places. But before the Great Western had opened, connecting railways were already being planned by other companies, to link with Exeter in the west, and Cheltenham and Gloucester via Swindon. Brunel's aim was not just to build a railway line, but to create a new railway system. The 'Railway Mania' of the 1840s and 1850s saw the British railway network

expand rapidly, and it was estimated that in 1845 over 200,000 people were employed in the building of railways all over the country.

By the time of Brunel's death in 1859, the GWR and associated companies stretched from London to Penzance in the West, and into West Wales through the South Wales Railway, of which he was also the engineer. The purchase of the West Midland Railway in 1863 brought the company into the West Midlands. By 1866 the company owned or worked 592 miles of broad gauge track, 240 miles of mixed gauge and 462 miles of standard gauge.

Although the railway had steadily grown in the nineteenth century, after grouping in 1923 the

The 'Lion & Wheel' totem adopted by British Railways immediately after the nationalisation of Britain's railways.

Navvies at work converting Brunel's broad gauge at Saltash Bridge.

Wartime conditions at Birmingham Snow Hill Station.

Great Western acquired large numbers of railways, particularly in South Wales. When the 'Big Four' railways of the Great Western, the Southern, The London Midland & Scottish and the London & North Eastern Railways, were created, the GWR was the only one of the new companies to keep its original name, making it one of the biggest and most prosperous railway companies in the world.

During the Second World War the 'Big Four' railways and London Transport had been under the control of the Railway Executive. After some debate, this arrangement was made permanent and in 1948 the Great Western Railway became part of British Railways when all four main line railway companies were nationalised by the government.

In the years after nationalisation, British Railways (Western Region) retained much of the character and traditions of the old Great Western. Much changed with the Beeching Report of 1963 which recommended the closure of many small stations and lines and reduced the size of the network by over 40%. Many staff lost their jobs, and small communities lost railways linking them with the rest of the country.

In recent years, the privatisation of British Rail has seen a return to a railway network run by many different railway companies. Today the track, stations and signalling of railways is looked after by Network Rail, and most of the train services on Brunel's old main line are provided by First Great Western, reintroducing the old name.

Operating the Railway - The Driver

Until recently, the ambition of many youngsters was to be an engine driver, and the job of engine driver was seen as the top job amongst railway staff. Becoming a driver of a large express engine like 'Caerphilly Castle' or 'King George V' did not happen overnight. Years of experience were needed before taking the controls of such an important locomotive. The bottom of the ladder was the job of engine cleaner, and boys wishing to become drivers started here.

Steam engines were dirty and oily and it was the job of the cleaner to not only keep the engines sparkling, but also to shovel out all the ash and clinker from the locomotive ash pan at the end of

the day. It was also the job of the most junior member of staff to go from the shed early in the morning to knock on the doors of drivers to ensure they got to work on time! Drivers then worked their way upward, starting as drivers on shunting engines, gradually working on more important services as they gained more experience.

Great skill was required to both drive and fire steam locomotives - there is a hands on exhibit near the Dean goods locomotive that shows that skill - the 'Train Driving' simulator.

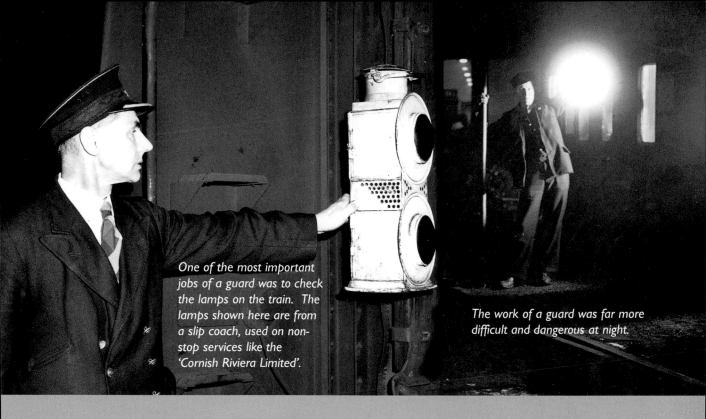

One of the most important jobs of a guard was to check the lamps on the train. The lamps shown here are from a slip coach, used on non-stop services like the 'Cornish Riviera Limited'.

The work of a guard was far more difficult and dangerous at night.

The Guard

Another significant, although more humble, job on the railway was that of the guard. The tasks carried out by passenger and goods guards were different, although the safety, security and correct operation of the train were common to both. Guards were responsible for the whole length of the train, except the engine itself, and details of every trip were kept and sent to divisional headquarters. Many guards came to know the sounds a train made as it passed under bridges or climbed hills, so they could tell their position on the route exactly. Guards carried special instructions and timetables to keep the train running correctly, and lamps and detonators to warn other trains in an emergency. Until more recent times, guards vans were a familiar sight, attached to the end of long goods trains as they

made their way along the line. With the advent of continuous braking systems, brake vans have become obsolete and with them the job of goods guard. The brake van seen here is a typical GWR design, built in 1946, known as a 'Toad' - all wagons used by the railway were allocated names to allow them to be identified in paperwork and telegraph messages. The wide veranda not only gave the guard a good view, but also housed the brake handle which was used by the guard to control the speed of the train where required. Inside the van as well as emergency equipment, the guard also had a stove, very useful on long winter nights when guards could spend lonely hours as the train made its way from station to station.

The Signalman

A view of the large signal box at Reading East around 1914. Most signal boxes had far fewer levers than the one shown here.

The signal box displayed is a replica of a small GWR signal cabin, and has been equipped with some of the original equipment a box of this size would have carried. The lever frame, which was used to change points or operate signals, came from Ladbroke Grove just outside of Paddington. The frame was modified by London Transport, which took over the box, which is why some of the original GWR features are now absent. In small signal boxes the signalman had a solitary life. Inside the box there were few facilities, often no running water or toilet, and only a small stove and kettle. Meals had to be taken during a break in the traffic. The floors and brass fittings were kept beautifully polished but no armchairs or

newspapers were allowed in case the signalman was distracted or fell asleep. Outside the box a variety of GWR signals are displayed, including a selection of the original signals from the broad gauge era - including a fantail, and disc and crossbar type, unique survivors of Brunel's railway.

The signalman had to know his systems exactly and be able to work under pressure, because a small mistake in signalling or controlling points could lead to disaster. In the early days of the GWR, long working hours and lack of sleep led to many accidents, but the Company resisted the use of mechanical aids, because they were thought to lead to lack of concentration.

An example of one of the electromechanical signal boxes introduced in the 1930s to replace the old style boxes.

From the 1860s to the 1880s, new safety devices were at last introduced. These prevented the wrong lever being pulled by mistake, and sent messages by telegraph or bell to allow only one train to travel on the line at a time.

Signalmen needed intensive training, learning much on the job, and regular examinations were taken to ensure staff were up to scratch. Modern signalling uses electronic switchboards, which have greatly increased comfort and convenience, and many manual signal boxes have now been removed. There are many more fail-safe systems but accidents can still occur.

A Goods Porter at Paddington Goods Depot in the 1920s.

Great Western Goods

Although the Great Western Railway transported thousands of passengers each year, the task of moving goods from place to place was just as important to the company. Although there is much less goods traffic carried by rail today, it remains an important mode of transport for heavy or bulk goods such as coal, stone or oil. In fact, goods traffic on railways has increased in recent years. Today there is far less variety in the items transported by rail. The large pile of goods displayed at the beginning of this section of the Museum illustrates the huge number of different items the railway did move in its heyday.

The work of the Shunter in the Goods Yard was highly skilled - wagons needed to be sorted into the right order and couplings hooked up and unhooked. The dangers lurking in a goods yard were considerable - shunters could be knocked over by wagons as they were propelled into sidings, or crushed between the buffers of wagons if a driver was not concentrating on what he was doing! Although in smaller goods yards horses were used to move wagons around, in larger stations small tank locomotives, such as 'Pannier Tank' No. 9400, were used to do the work. The wagon next to No. 9400 is known as a 'Shunter's Truck' and was used by shunters to ride around larger goods yards in safety. The toolbox on top of the wagon was used to store spare couplings and shunters' poles, the 'tool of the trade' for shunters - the character figure between the buffers is holding one of these too.

The scale of the coal traffic handled by the GWR can be seen in this view of one of the many goods yards in the South Wales area.

The wide variety of wagons used by the GWR can be seen in this view of Acton Yard, taken to mark the testing of the first 100 wagon train on the Great Western in 1904.

As well as moving goods from station to station, the Great Western and British Railways ran a service to deliver goods from the station to the customer. Once unloaded from the goods wagon, the goods could be stored in the Goods Shed in the station yard. Once the paperwork had been completed, goods could either be collected by the customer or delivered by the Great Western's own staff. From the earliest days this was done by horse-drawn vehicles, and the dray seen here was used in the Bristol area for many years. Horses were cheaper to run than lorries for short runs where much time was spent waiting around. This is why 500 GWR horses still worked in London as late as 1937, even though the first lorry was in use in 1905. The new lorries could do in eight hours what horses had done in 14. In 1933, express parcel vans were introduced in London. They

carried cream, fish, live animals and food that would not keep - very useful in the days before freezers. Fresh fish from Cornwall, which arrived at Paddington Station at 4.00pm, could be delivered to a restaurant, in time to be served the same evening.

The 'mechanical horse' on display here is typical of many used all over Britain in all manner of locations, and although it was not originally owned by the GWR, its livery has been carefully researched to illustrate the type carried by other GWR vehicles of the period. The GWR goods wagon is a 'Mink' wagon used to carry general goods and produce. Other specialist wagons were used to transport things like fish, bananas, milk and grain and all had weird and wonderful names like 'Bloaters', 'Micas' and 'Mogos'!

A view of Paddington Station with passengers awaiting the departure of the 'Cornish Riviera Limited' express.

Passenger Travel

Thousands of people travelled on trains across the Great Western network each day. Some journeys were business, others for pleasure, with many using the railway to visit the seaside for their annual holiday.

Today, far fewer people use trains, but the number is again increasing. Although steam locomotives no longer haul them, modern trains are faster and more comfortable than they were.
With the introduction of services such as Eurostar, fast international travel is now possible.

The station building on our platform is a replica, based on a number of real locations, including Eynsham in Oxfordshire, Culkerton in Gloucestershire and Banbury in Oxfordshire.
It is typical of the smaller stations all over the GWR network, whose humble appearance contrasted with the grand stations like those at Paddington, Birmingham Snow Hill and Bristol Temple Meads.

Today buying a ticket at a railway station is very simple - you can even buy tickets over the phone or the Internet! In the golden age of steam, passengers were required to buy their tickets at ticket offices like this one in our station. The booking clerk sat behind the wooden partition, surrounded by racks containing all the numerous tickets he might require. Depending on what sort of journey you might take, or what type of passenger you might be, there were hundreds of

different tickets - First, Second or Third Class, Single or Return, Excursion or Day Return. There were tickets for the transport of dogs, and even if you were a shipwrecked sailor, there was a ticket for you! Tickets were also required if you wanted to stand on station platforms - until the introduction of 'open stations' you needed a platform ticket. Why not try out one of our platform ticket machines?

Refreshment Rooms at
Exeter St Davids Station
in the 1930s.

Reading Refreshment Rooms around 1914.

Many of the jokes about curled up railway sandwiches date from the early days of railway catering! Before the Great Western ran its own refreshment rooms, it leased them to private companies who did not always treat passengers well in those early days. The Swindon refreshment rooms were no exception, and there were many complaints about the standard of food served. Brunel complained about the coffee, and you can hear his letter of complaint in this display. Things were so bad that Swindon was nicknamed 'Swindleum' by irate travellers who only had 10 minutes to eat their refreshments. Happily in later years things improved, and passengers could take refreshment from a variety of sources - refreshment trolleys like the one shown here, refreshment rooms, and buffet and dining cars on the trains themselves. Today thankfully, the standard of food served on trains and at stations is rather better than in the past - usually!

The Clockmakers Workshop at Reading Signal Works. All clocks and watches used by the Great Western, apart from those at Swindon Works, were maintained here.

One of the Ticket Offices at Birmingham Snow Hill Station in 1913.

The coming of railways also brought a revolution in the way in which we tell the time. Before the railways came, every town and city relied on its own local time, and there was a wide difference between one side of the country and the other. In order to run trains to a timetable, a standard time for the whole country was needed, and, largely as a result of pressure from railway companies, Greenwich Mean Time was introduced. Clocks were a feature of all GWR stations and offices, and a time signal was transmitted by telegraph once a week to ensure that all clocks told the same time. The Railway had a clock workshop at Reading Signal Works that maintained the thousands of clocks and watches used by the company and its staff, some of which are on display in the showcase.

Speed to The West

From the end of the Victorian era onwards, more and more ordinary people could afford to take a holiday or day trip by rail. The Great Western Railway responded by successfully promoting itself as 'The Holiday Line'.

No other railway company matched the quality and output of the Great Western's publicity material. Their historical books, popular guides and striking posters offered people a compelling and romantic image of the company's holiday regions. For the manual workers, craftsmen and huge new class of office workers in Britain's congested and smoky towns, 'Smiling Somerset', 'Glorious Devon' and the 'Cornish Riviera' seemed full of promise.

In order to attract passengers during the quiet season, the GWR went to great lengths to promote Cornwall as a winter holiday resort. One publication noted "The blessings of warmth, sunshine and a mild climate may be found during the winter months without crossing the channel or the continent or incurring the toil and expense of a sojourn in Egypt, a visit to Algiers or even a trip to Nice or San Remo". GWR tourism had an enormous impact on the once remote regions of Devon and Cornwall. The influx of thousands of visitors every year quickly turned Torquay, Newquay, Penzance and St.Ives into prime resorts, with many other towns to follow. In 1906 the 'Daily Telegraph' reported 'scarcely a place on the coast untouched by the ramifications of Brunel's famous line'. Passengers taking advantage of tourist-rate tickets flocked to the beaches while shops and businesses sprang up to cater for this new wave of holidaymakers. Local people took in lodgers during the holiday season and the GWR opened its own prestigious hotels and rented out camping facilities in old railway carriages for those on a tighter budget.

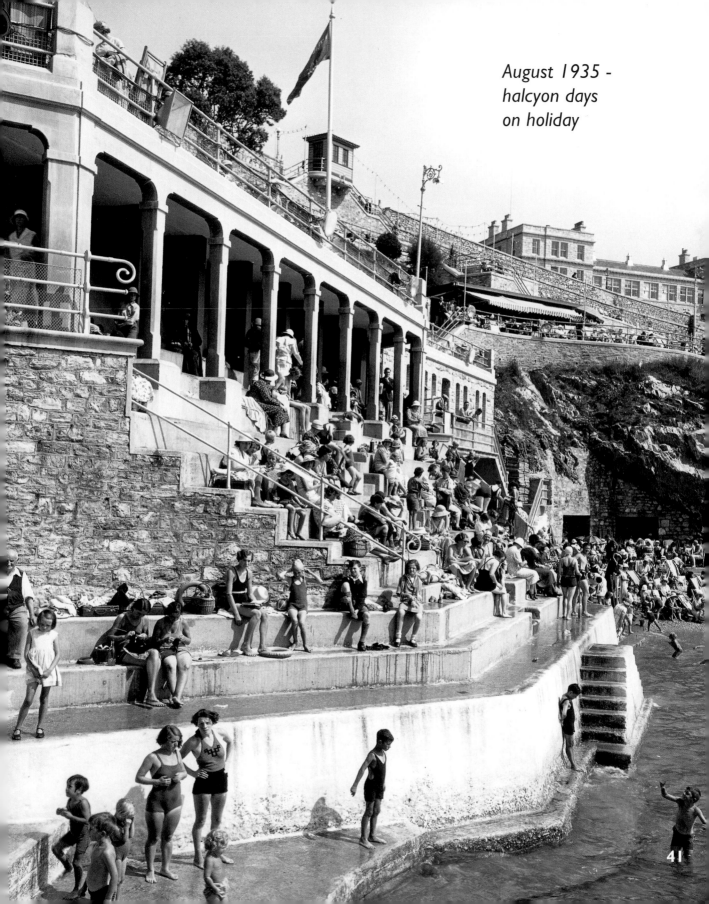

August 1935 -
halcyon days
on holiday

41

The Great Western used buses to advertise their services. Many travelled huge distances. In the period before 1914, buses were sent to Scotland and the North of England, deep into the heart of their rival's territory.

Holidaymakers arriving at another popular GWR destination, Weston-super-Mare.

The bookstall at Paddington Station. GWR books and pamphlets are much in evidence in this 1913 view.

A view of one of GWR's hotels .

After nationalisation BR Western Region continued to produce posters for the old Great Western resorts but, despite their efforts, the number of people taking holidays by train steadily decreased. The rise of car ownership was the single biggest factor in that decline. The car gave families a sense of freedom, flexibility and privacy that seemed unanswerable. Packed holiday trains were increasingly replaced by busy roads to the coast. Today, the popularity of English resorts has faded like the holiday trains before them. Many of today's holidaymakers head for the airport and resorts overseas.

Speed, comfort and glamour were the hallmarks of the Great Western's holiday express trains epitomised by the 'Cornish Riviera Ltd.' and the 'Torbay Express'. Whether you were taking a third class ticket on a packed excursion train to Weymouth or travelling first class on the 'Cornish Riviera', the GWR aimed to provide as fast and as comfortable a service as possible. Extra trains were laid on to cater for the increasing numbers of holidaymakers and day-trippers taking advantage of the GWR's cut price Holiday Season Tickets. Improvements to the old main line between Paddington and Penzance meant passengers for Devon and Cornwall could expect to reach their destination in record time.

The 'Cornish Riviera Ltd.' was the GWR's most prestigious holiday train. Introduced in 1904, the train provided passengers with a faster, more comfortable and convenient service than ever before. The 'Torbay Express' began its historic runs from Paddington to Torbay in the 1920s. By 1938, at peak periods each train could carry over 1,000 people to the resorts of South Devon. In August Bank Holiday weekend of that year, 20,000 people arrived in Torquay alone from London, Wales, Bristol, and the Midlands. With the trains so packed, not everyone was lucky enough to get a seat.

Day-trippers and holidaymakers stepping down from packed Great Western Trains expected to enjoy a more active holiday than many people choose today. Early trippers arrived at the seaside laden with coats, umbrellas, buckets, spades and baskets of food.

By the end of the 19th century, big resorts like Torquay and Weymouth entertained the crowds with sideshows, donkey rides, brass bands and boat rides. Dances and concerts in glamorous pavilions all added to the holiday fun. Those who preferred a more peaceful time could opt for the smaller bays and fishing ports served by the GWR's branch lines and motorbuses. In the 1920s and 30s GWR literature recommended sightseeing, rambling, cycling, and golf as alternatives to the big seaside resorts. Although many holidaymakers could only afford to stay in boarding houses or lodgings, the better off could stay at one of the company's own hotels. As well as the prestigious Great Western Hotel at Paddington, the railway also owned three others, all providing a very high standard of accommodation.

Swindon Trip Holiday

Every year, Swindon Works closed for ten days and the company ferried its employees and their families to their chosen holiday destination. It was a massive operation and by 1912 it involved moving almost 25,000 people on 23 different trains.

In order to dispatch all the trippers promptly, the long haul trains bound for Cornwall left Swindon on the evening the factory closed. Early next morning, Swindon trippers poured onto the sidings, walking along the railway tracks to where their trains lay waiting.

One publicity campaign run by the GWR was that Cornwall was warm enough for 'Bathing In February'.

Many people have happy childhood memories of travelling by train to the seaside.

'Trip' tickets could be used to travel almost anywhere on the British railway network, although many Swindon families chose familiar destinations such as Weston-Super-Mare and Barry Island. Most popular of all were the trains that ran to Weymouth where the influx of railway families was so great the town became known as 'Swindon-by-the-Sea'. With its workforce gone, Swindon itself was left strangely empty, and many other businesses in the town closed during trip week since trade was so poor. Also, everyone knew that money was tight after Trip Week. Until 1938 holidays were unpaid, so many Swindon families came home early or spent just a day away.

The Workshop

This part of the building was added in 1929 and 1930, when parts of Brunel's original workshops were demolished and both the building that is now the Museum, and the old 'B' Shed next door, were extended. The newer brickwork can be clearly seen on the 1872 stone wall.

On the back wall of the gallery is the 'Swindon Works Wall of Names' – a tribute to the many thousands of people who worked in the Great Western in the Swindon area. Members of their family, or friends, who through a contribution to the Swindon Railway Heritage Trust, have pledged each name. If you would like to nominate someone for the 'Wall of Names', Please contact the Museum and ask for the relevant form.

A viewing gallery overlooking the main Bristol to London railway line is next to the 'Wall of Names', giving views of modern rolling stock on Brunel's original Great Western line.

Museum Information

Opening Times

The Museum is open all year
10.00am to 5.00pm daily.
The Museum is closed 25 and 26 December
and 1 January.

Group Visits

Groups of 15 or more need to be booked in
advance to qualify for group discount rates.
Telephone 01793 466637 for details.

Corporate Hire

STEAM is a unique venue for business meetings
and corporate events.
Telephone 01793 466619 for details.

Educational Visits

We welcome school visits and we have a range of
packages and resources available for educational
and school visits. Telephone 01793 466640 for
details.

The Museum Shop

STEAM has a well-stocked shop selling a range of
books, videos, gifts and souvenirs.

The STEAM Picture Library

STEAM's picture library offers a wealth of images
covering industrial engineering and social history,
country views and people, as well as locomotives,
trains and rolling stock. And it's available to you.
Telephone 01793 466607 for details.

Disabled Access

We are proud that **STEAM** is fully accessible.
If you have any special requirements, please
telephone 01793 466646.

Friends of Swindon Railway Museum

The Friends actively support the Museum,
providing practical assistance and help. The Friends
also run an interesting programme of talks and
lectures throughout the year. For more details,
contact the Friends Secretary, c/o **STEAM** –
Museum of the Great Western Railway.

Original Text by Tim Bryan - 2000
Updated by Jeff Salter - 2005

Photography by Peter Smith of Newbery Smith Photography

Additional pictures from the **STEAM** Picture Library and the National Railway Museum, York

Designed and published by Heritage House Group Ltd, Heritage House, Lodge Lane, Derby DE1 3HE
Tel: 01332 347087   Fax: 01332 290688   Email: publications@hhgroup.co.uk

HERITAGE HOUSE
Group Limited